PRIMATES

BONOBOS

BY TRUDY BECKER

WWW.APEXEDITIONS.COM

Apex is distributed by North Star Editions:
sales@northstareditions.com | 888-417-0195

Produced for Apex by Red Line Editorial.

Photographs ©: Shutterstock Images, cover, 1, 4–5, 10–11, 12, 13, 14–15, 16–17, 18–19, 20–21, 24–25, 26–27, 28–29; Sunday Berlioz Kakpo/iNaturalist, 6; iStockphoto, 7, 8, 22–23

Library of Congress Control Number: 2025939159

ISBN
979-8-89250-794-3 (hardcover)
979-8-89250-823-0 (paperback)
979-8-89250-879-7 (ebook pdf)
979-8-89250-852-0 (hosted ebook)

Printed in the United States of America
Mankato, MN
012026

NOTE TO PARENTS AND EDUCATORS

Apex books are designed to build literacy skills in striving readers. Exciting, high-interest content attracts and holds readers' attention. The text is carefully leveled to allow students to achieve success quickly. Additional features, such as bolded glossary words for difficult terms, help build comprehension.

TABLE OF CONTENTS

CHAPTER 1

FINDING FRUIT

A group of bonobos moves through the trees. They swing from branch to branch. The bonobos are hungry. They are searching for fruit.

Bonobos can grip branches with their toes as they climb.

One bonobo finds a velvet tamarind tree. Fruit fills its branches. The bonobo jumps toward it. He makes a loud noise.

Velvet tamarinds are small brown fruits. They are about the size of grapes.

Fruit makes up more than half of what a bonobo eats.

FOOD FUN

Bonobos get excited when they find something good to eat. The more they like it, the higher they squeal. They may chase and play with one another, too.

The other bonobos hear him. The apes rush to the same spot. They grab the fruit and gulp it down. They hoot and squeal as they eat.

FAST FACT

Bonobos often share food with one another.

Bonobos don't need to drink much. They mainly get water from the food they eat.

CHAPTER 2

ALL ABOUT BONOBOS

Bonobos are a type of great ape. Great apes are **primates** with big bodies and large brains. Adult male bonobos can weigh up to 86 pounds (39 kg).

Most bonobos are around 3 feet (0.9 m) tall.

When on all fours, bonobos fold their hands into fists. They walk on their knuckles.

A bonobo's fur is black. A tuft of white appears on its bottom. Bonobos mainly walk on all fours. But they are also good at walking on two legs.

CLOSE FAMILY

Bonobos are close **relatives** of chimpanzees. Their **DNA** is more than 99 percent similar. Bonobos are closely related to humans, too. Their DNA is nearly 99 percent the same.

Bonobos used to be called "pygmy chimpanzees" because they look like small chimps.

Bonobos sleep in the nests they make.

Bonobos live in rainforests. They are found in just one country. It is the Democratic Republic of the Congo.

FAST FACT

Bonobos live near the Congo River. They build leafy nests in trees.

CHAPTER 3

LIFE IN THE WILD

Bonobos mostly eat fruit. They also munch on leaves and seeds. But they may sometimes eat small animals.

Bonobos may eat plant stalks and shoots.

Bonobos often travel in groups of 6 to 15 when searching for food.

Every day, bonobos spend hours searching for food. They go out in small groups. Bonobos find some food on the rainforest floor. Other food grows high up in the **canopy**.

FAST FACT

Some bonobos wash their food in streams.

Bonobos **communicate** with one another in many ways. They use their hands, faces, and voices. Bonobos make certain sounds when having fun. They make other noises when danger is near.

FACING DANGER

Human actions have hurt bonobos. Some people hunt the apes. Others cut down trees in their **habitat**. Nearby wars have harmed bonobos, too. As a result, the apes are **endangered**.

In the 2020s, fewer than 20,000 bonobos lived in the wild.

CHAPTER 4

LIFE CYCLE

Bonobos are **social** animals. They live in large groups called troops. Troops usually have more than 30 members.

Some bonobo troops have more than 100 members.

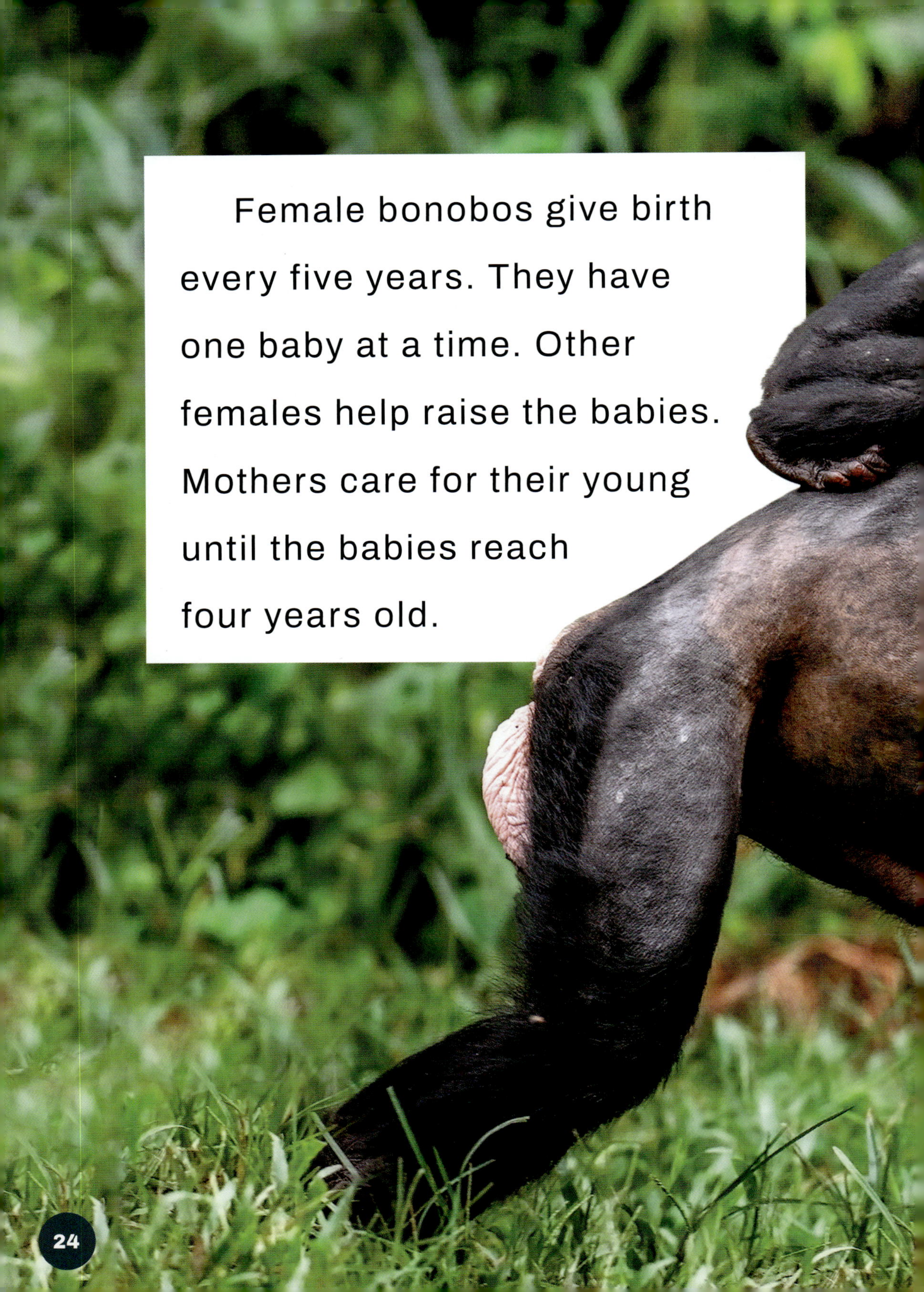

Female bonobos give birth every five years. They have one baby at a time. Other females help raise the babies. Mothers care for their young until the babies reach four years old.

For the first few years, bonobo mothers carry their babies on their backs.

IN CHARGE

Female bonobos usually lead troops. They make decisions for their groups. For example, they may choose when and where the troops travel.

Bonobos begin having babies at about 14 years old.

Once fully grown, females leave their troops. They join new ones. Males stay with their mothers. They remain in the same troops for life.

FAST FACT

Bonobos usually live 20 to 40 years in the wild.

COMPREHENSION QUESTIONS

Write your answers on a separate piece of paper.

1. Write a few sentences explaining the main ideas of Chapter 4.

2. What fact about bonobos did you find most interesting? Why?

3. What is the main food that bonobos eat?

- **A.** small animals
- **B.** leaves
- **C.** fruit

4. How would cutting down trees harm bonobos?

- **A.** The apes would have too much space.
- **B.** The apes would have less food and shelter.
- **C.** The apes would have to make bigger nests.

5. What does **related** mean in this book?

*Bonobos are closely **related** to humans, too. Their DNA is nearly 99 percent the same.*

- **A.** similar
- **B.** different
- **C.** colorful

6. What does **decisions** mean in this book?

*They make **decisions** for their groups. For example, they may choose when and where the troops travel.*

- **A.** choices
- **B.** food
- **C.** nests

Answer key on page 32.

GLOSSARY

canopy
A dense layer of leaves and branches high up in trees.

communicate
To send and receive messages.

DNA
A chemical in the body that shapes how creatures look and grow.

endangered
In danger of dying out forever.

habitat
The type of place where animals normally live.

primates
Animals in a group that includes apes and monkeys.

relatives
Animals that are similar because they come from the same earlier group.

social
Likely to spend time with other animals of the same type.

TO LEARN MORE

BOOKS

Duling, Kaitlyn. *Mountain Gorillas*. Bellwether Media, 2021.

Huddleston, Emma. *Thank You, Primates*. The Child's World, 2022.

Rains, Dalton. *Chimpanzees*. Apex Editions, 2025.

ONLINE RESOURCES

Visit **www.apexeditions.com** to find links and resources related to this title.

ABOUT THE AUTHOR

Trudy Becker lives in Minneapolis, Minnesota. She likes exploring new places and loves anything involving books.

INDEX

ANSWER KEY:
1. Answers will vary; 2. Answers will vary; 3. C; 4. B; 5. A; 6. A